What Is a
Scientist?

This book is dedicated to my son, Scott Chamberlin, who introduced me to the joys of scientific investigation, and to my husband, Doug Chamberlin, for his unwavering encouragement.

—B.L.

To Lisa and Jocelyn

—C.K.

Special thanks to the first grade scientists at

Willard School in Concord, MA, who appear in this book.

Text copyright © 1998 by Barbara Lehn
Photographs copyright © 1998 by Carol Krauss

Millbrook Press
A division of Lerner Publishing Group, Inc.
241 First Avenue North
Minneapolis, MN 55401 USA

For reading levels and more information, look up this title at www.lernerbooks.com.

Library of Congress Cataloging-in-Publication Data
Lehn, Barbara.
What is a scientist? / Barbara Lehn; photographs by Carol Krauss. p. cm.
Summary: Simple text and photographs depict children engaged in various activities that make up the scientific process.
ISBN 978–0–7613–1272–7 (lib. bdg. : alk. paper)
ISBN 978–0–7613–8084–9 (EB pdf)
1. Scientists—Vocational guidance—Pictorial works—Juvenile literature.
[1. Scientists—Vocational guidance. 2. Vocational guidance.] I. Krauss, Carol, ill. II. Title.
Q-147.L444   1998
502.3—DC21   98-13984

Manufactured in the United States of America
23-46801-337-10/25/2018

What Is a Scientist?

Barbara Lehn

Photographs by Carol Krauss

M Millbrook Press • Minneapolis

A scientist is
a person who
asks questions
and tries different
ways to answer
them.

Hannah wonders about fruits and vegetables.

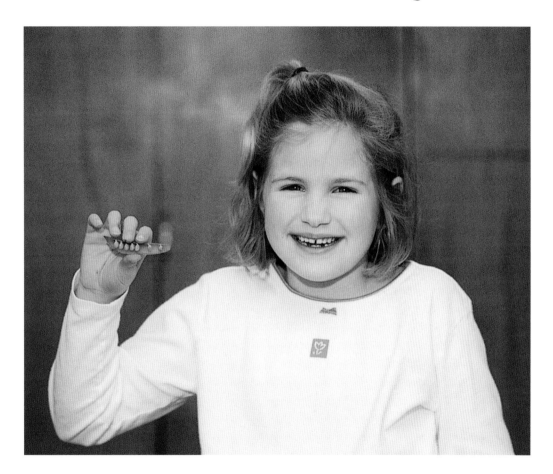

"Are there this many peas in *every* pea pod?" asks Hannah.

A scientist **learns** from her **senses**.

Cami and Tiara play with a mixture of water and cornstarch. They try to decide if it is liquid or solid.

"When I squeeze it, it feels like a solid, but it drips like a liquid!" observes Tiara.

A scientist
notices details.

Nate
examines
seeds inside
vegetables.

"There are
actually *two*
kinds of seeds
in the cucumber.
The small ones
are clear,"
discovers Nate.

A scientist **draws** what she **sees**.

Samantha shows how two liquids mix.

"The red drops beaded up inside the yellow liquid," observes Samantha.

A scientist **writes** about what **happens**.

Tim
records his
observation.

"The checker
and pencil
landed at
the same
time, but
not the
feather,"
writes Tim.

A scientist makes **comparisons** by **measuring**.

Amelia and Corey are measuring weights with the balance scale.

"Amelia, this side of the balance is higher because it is lighter," demonstrates Corey.

A scientist must **count exactly**.

Emily and Stewart count how many drops of water they can fit on a penny.

"We've put on 23 drops of water so far," says Emily.

A scientist looks at objects carefully to **decide** how to **sort**.

Zoe and her group organize the shoes and boots in different ways.

"You guys, I think this boot is longer," decides Zoe.

A scientist **designs experiments** to **test predictions**.

Jessie plants seeds at the top of one cup and the bottom of another.

"I think the seeds that I planted at the top will grow better than the ones at the bottom," predicts Jessie.

A scientist experiments by **trial and error**.

Nick uses a foam meat tray to make a flying object.

"I added a blob of clay and some paper clips on the front, and now my meat tray flies farther," explains Nick.

A scientist **thinks** **logically**.

Shivani explains how she learned about the compass directions.

"When I ride home at the end of the day, the sun is going down over there, so that must be west," figures Shivani.

A scientist **keeps trying** over and over.

Charlie and Stewart try to build a tower as tall as possible.

"Stewart, we finally got more than ten to stay on!" shouts Charlie.

A scientist **has fun**.

Jeff and Theresa experiment with water.

"Let's see if we can fill up the tube through these holes," suggests Jeff.

A scientist is a person who...

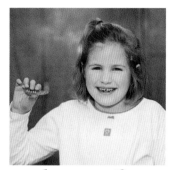

asks questions

learns from her senses

notices details

draws

writes

measures

counts

sorts

tests predictions

experiments

thinks logically

keeps trying

and has fun.

That's what a **scientist** is!

About the **Author** and **Photographer**

Barbara Lehn has been involved in regular and special education for more than 25 years. She currently teaches hands-on science in her first grade class in Concord, Massachusetts. She wrote this book to help young children understand that they are scientists and to appreciate that they engage in scientific inquiry naturally and joyously. Barbara lives in Andover, Massachusetts, with her husband and son.

Carol Krauss turned to professional photography after a career in management consulting. Her black and white fine-art photographs have been shown in a variety of New England galleries. *What Is a Scientist?* is her first book project. She divides her time between Massachusetts and California.